Michael Winicott

I0488703

STEVE JOBS: BUSINESS LESSONS

Teachings from the most successful innovator in the world

© 2015 by Michael Winicott.

© 2015 by UNITEXTO

Published by UNITEXTO

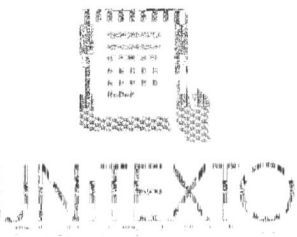

TABLE OF CONTENTS

INTRODUCTION

One of the largest corporations in the world is Apple Incorporated. Using innovative technology from one of the greatest masterminds in the world, Apple has created a new world of instruments and tools that have drastically changed the world and the way we interact with. Were it not for the dreams and aspirations of Steve Jobs, the world of internet technology and communications would be very different.

Steve Jobs was one of the greatest entrepreneurs to have ever lived, and with his insight and experiences you too can learn how to fulfill your dreams. This book will go deep into the business that Jobs took from the ground up to create an international company that creates revenues of hundreds of billions of dollars. You will be following in the footsteps of one of the greatest innovators in Silicon Valley, and will learn what made Steve Jobs so great.

The business and leadership lessons that Jobs will show you will open the doors of opportunity for your life and your goals. With every chapter, we will be focusing on not only building your dream, but on building you as a person to create a mastermind entrepreneur. Not only was Steve Jobs one of the most successful men in his industry, but he also dealt with some of the most challenging obstacles that come with starting and running a business. Preparing yourself through the eyes of Jobs will create a foundation within you that will spark your innovation, exhilarate your creativity, and culture a lifestyle within you that will speed up the productivity you have towards reaching your dreams.

Apply Incorporated started out as a small company that turned into the industry's leading international corporation that supplies technology to the world. How did Steve Jobs create the iPhone from thin air, and integrate technologies that would open a market for app makers all over the world to share their ideas with others? It is incredible how Jobs opened his mind to the possibilities of tomorrow, and focused his business to show to the world what he could do.

As an entrepreneur, it is important to understand that your world is the playground on which you can create anything that you desire. Because Steve Jobs followed this, he became one of the most successful men in the world, and he is now known in every household in America. Entrepreneurial greatness is not something that you are born with, but through hard work, diligent preparation, and a process of failure, your eyes can be open to a path that will forever change your life.

Let us begin the journey through the pieces of greatness that put together the mind of Steve Jobs.

Through his trials and triumphs, we will see how he unfolded his masterpiece, and created a company that never would have been possible if it weren't for the foundation of his entrepreneurial mastermind.

THE LIFE OF STEVE JOBS

Childhood Years

The background that created one of the most powerful men on Earth was exceptional and unique. The life that Jobs lived was unlike most people, and the synopsis of this chapter will show just how truly magnificent he was under the circumstances that he was given. The journey begins with his birth in San Francisco, California. His parents, two University of Wisconsin Graduate Students, quickly gave Steve Jobs up for adoption, and he was adopted by Clara and Paul Jobs.

Paul's interest in machinery and electronics was passed down to Steve Jobs through small projects that they handled together. Constructing and tinkering with various electronic devices grew Job's interest in what will eventually become his industry. His adopted father cultured and strengthened Steve's interest and skill in pulling apart and reassembling those electronics, and with this innovator's mindset Steve Jobs began to mold into his entrepreneurial greatness.

His highly intelligent mind caused both advanced learning, and he moved through his high school years at the top of the list. During his high school years he met his future partner, Steve Wozniak, and the relationship of a century began to grow into the powerful partnership that later created Apple Computers.

Post-College Years

Steve Jobs graduated from high school and enrolled into Reed College in Portland, Oregon, but shortly realized that this was not the path that he was meant to take. Dissatisfied with the structure of college, Jobs dropped out of college after 6 months, and instead attended classes that interested him for the next 18 months, attending them strictly for gaining pure knowledge. This decision to attend these creative classes armed him with the interests and passions that later took his company into the industry as he did.

With an underlying knowledge molded from his childhood and his friendship with Steve Wozniak, Steve Jobs entered into the computer industry. However, he entered it humbly as a video game designer for Atari, but quickly left the employment after about 6 months. From there, Steve made the decision to adventure to India in exploration of himself. This personal meditation period was filled with reflection, travelling, and experimentation with many drugs that were available in India at the time.

The Creation of Apple

On his return from India, Jobs and Wozniak created their legendary company, Apple Computers. The set up was highly makeshift, with their operations

10

being held in their garage. The mission of Apple Computers was to create electronics that would be cheaper, smaller, and much more intuitive than the standard black-and-white style computer available on the market in those times. Wozniak was the electronic genius behind the computers in the beginning, with Jobs in charge of marketing their efforts to sell their first model, the Apple I.

With over $700,000 in earnings after one year of creating the company with the Apple I, things quickly began to evolve into Job's favor. The sales of Apple Computers rose, and soon the Apple II was on the market. By 1980, Apple Computers became a publicly traded company, with its incorporation being well over $1 billion in market value after just its first day.

However, as the company became incorporated, Jobs began to see his standing with the company that he created become less safe. With some slumping sales against the mega-company IBM, Apple Computers President John Sculley began to push Steve Jobs out of the company, claiming that he was hurting the growth of the company. By 1984, Steve Jobs no longer had control or a standing position within the company that he co-founded with Steve Wozniak. With the mind of an innovator, Steve Jobs took the hit of losing his company and moved on to continue creating.

From Apple to Apple

After his control over Apple Computers was lost, Jobs moved on in search of more investment opportunities. In 1985, Jobs began his own software enterprise called NeXT, Inc. and in the following year an animation company was bought from George Lucas by Steve Jobs which would later become Pixar Animation Studios. With these two new companies to focus on, he immediately went to work in increasing their value.

While Pixar was creating value for Jobs, his project with NeXT was not yielding such success. His specialized operating systems were not breaking through and growing the company as he wished, and in 1996 his original company bought NeXT from Jobs for $429 million. However, with this, Jobs soon took back his post as Apple's CEO, and began his acceleration of the company as he did before in the 1980's. With his original company back in his hands, the operations of Apple Computers changed drastically back into the innovative and creative operations that took place during Steve Job's control of the company in 1984.

The High Life of Jobs

Steve Jobs integrated a new management system, and changed the operations that would contribute to Apple's magnificent success in the 1990's and into the 21st century. His substantial efforts in the company's success caused an acceleration in the company's profits to something interstellar. The shares of the company inside the stock market was record breaking in the 2000's, and the revenue symbolized the extreme innovation that Steve Jobs created within Silicon Valley. His products became the new technology of the world, which lead the remaining companies around the world to follow in his genius.

Along with Apple's incredible success, Pixar Animation Studios produced some of the most well-known animated films of the century, bringing Pixar over $4 billion dollars in revenue. Disney merged with Pixar Animation Studios in 2006, making Steve Jobs not only the CEO of the largest and most successful technology company in the world, but also the largest shareholder in Disney and Pixar's massive incorporation.

The Personal Moments

Jobs fought through many battles of pancreatic cancer, but was finally overcome by the strength of the cancer in 2011. His personal life was immensely separated from the high-life of business that he lived in, and much of what went on in the personal life of Steve Jobs was not disclosed until after his death.

LEADERSHIP LESSON #1: PURSUE DREAMS, EVEN IT IS HARD

Steve Jobs held a very passionate interest in the industry of electronics and computer technology. However, although his interest was great, the actual entrance into such a large, mystifying and complex industry would be an impossible task that could never be taken on by a man who had dropped out of college. Steve Jobs wished to pursue one of the hardest industries in the world and make it to the top. Why did he succeed?

Steve's Solution

Steve Jobs did not take these facts about this industry and allow it to hurt his confidence or shut down that option. Instead, Jobs took the knowledge that this industry would be nearly impossible to enter, and he used that as the fuel for which he created his company. He did not listen to the words of his peers, or of the fears in his mind which told him to go the easy route. Steve Jobs could have stayed with Atari as a video game developer, and done very well in a career there, but Steve Jobs pursued what he was told he could not do.

Pursue the Stars, Not the Clouds

Jobs had several other options he could have taken that would have been easier than what he did.

However, he was not a man to listen to society, or to take the easy route to achieve things in an easy manner. Even with the knowledge that entering into the computer technology industry was complex and difficult, Jobs still pressed and fought for his spot among the greatest companies in that industry. His mindset was not about what was easy and quick, but about what was difficult, and a challenge that would take effort and hard work.

Steve Jobs pursued what others told him he could not. He pursued what was hard, and created a company out of the ashes of hard work and diligence. Could it be imagined how different the world would be if Steve Jobs had decided to take the easier route in life, instead of making the technological innovations that he did with his mind? People like Jobs who go above and beyond their lives, and who hunt for something greater than what they have, make a successful life, and change the world.

Summary

You have two choices with every problem that you face in life. You can take the easy route and yield the small rewards that come with being complacent, or you can decide to go your own way, build your own path, and fight upstream into a river that leads to gold. Though the road may be hard, pursuing the difficult means that you are one of a few that are pursuing it, and the rewards for your effort are large and endless. Taking the easy way out can be done by anyone, but making the decision to pursue more in your life is one that takes bravery and determination.

LEADERSHIP LESSON #2: FIND THE EDUCATION THAT WORKS FOR YOU

The academic prowess of Jobs was known long before he even entered high school. During his grade school years, his adopted parents were given the option to move Jobs up into high school because he tested so high on the school tests. However, although Steve Jobs was arguably one of the most intelligent human beings of his time, when he attended Reed College after high school, things didn't quite fit as he had expected. Why does a man who could have attended high school in 4th grade have such a disinterest in the education provided by the college he attended?

Steve's Solution

Although it's culturally unacceptable for someone to drop out of college, Steve Jobs did it anyway. For Jobs, the type of education provided by American college wasn't what he was looking for. He didn't want to take classes that he didn't want to take, and he felt that he wasn't learning as much as he could have. He instead took classes on his own and for no credit, and established his own grounds for education. He learned what he wanted to learn and how he wanted to learn it, and because of that decision, he became a multi-billion dollar man.

Educate Yourself How You Need it

The world has an unfortunate reputation towards people who don't go to college, labelling them as less intelligent and decreasing their job opportunities because of it. That myth is far from the truth, because college is simply a type of education. As someone who wishes to grow, education should be adopted and adapted to what can be easily digested, and bring the maximum value for the time that was taken out to learn the material.

Jobs did this by going his own way, and learning what he needed to learn. He educated himself in the classes that interested him, and he chose to make his education real, instead of simply fighting for credit that goes towards a college degree. College and education are two different things, because education requires effort, but attending college only requires money. Steve's education was not college, but attending classes, working for Atari, travelling through India in self-discovery. True education of the mind and the person comes from anywhere, and it is only a matter of how it's taken that affects how it educates.

Summary

You do not need education from college to become someone amazing. Education is a complex figure that is hidden among the many experiences in life. There is no limit to the availability and cost of education. The great thing about education is that it comes in your own form, and can be taken as strongly or as lightly as you wish to have it. Take Steve's advice, and pursue your own education based on what you need, not on what the world needs of you. Living life in this manner will open your eyes to how you are different, and how your place in the world can evolve into something astonishing.

LEADERSHIP LESSON #3: LEADERS FIND THEMSELVES

Being a leader requires an extreme sense of awareness that goes beyond just assumptions and peer evaluations. A leader must be a master of himself, and have the reins on every decision that is made towards success. This requires meditation, evaluation, understanding, and the adaptability to take the information that is found and taking action to culture the strengths and reinforce the weaknesses that are identified. Steve Jobs was a man of high intelligence, but he needed to understand his own mind in order to create the success that would become Apple Computers.

Steve's Solution

Knowing that he needed to have a deeper understanding of his own personality, Jobs took matters into his own hands by taking his adventure in India. He disregarded his job at Atari, because he understood the importance of self-reflection and understanding. He mastered himself by travelling in a place away from his old life, and coming to an understanding of who he is and what he can do. He halted his current affairs, left his old life behind, and pursued meditation in a place where nothing took place but his experiences with himself. There he molded into a man of himself.

An Understanding of Your Own Mind is Key

All of the education in the world is useless if there is no education in the person who is using it. While academic education is important, as well as skills and abilities that bring success, the truest form of education is of the mind, and the ability to identify ways to become harmonious with the actions and decisions that are made. Leaders must make this a priority, and even if the dreams they pursue is set back for a time, they must charge forward in search of themselves.

No leader can be successful if he does not know himself, because those who look up to him will not be able to know him either. Harmony requires precision and flawless fluidity between two parties. A leader cannot be harmonious with his team or his market if he does not understand a precise meaning behind himself. Doing whatever it takes to discover oneself will be a life changing experience that will not only bring a deeper understanding of the decisions that are made, but it might even change the course of the dreams and goals that were once originally made.

Summary

You must know yourself to know others, and to pursue the affairs of others. No business leader can succeed unless he is able to connect his mind with his decisions, and his decisions with the affects it has on people. Being connected to your own mind and body will bring you peace, make you more efficient as a leader, and will enable you to grow and expand your mind to further heights than you ever could have imagined before discovering yourself. All it takes is following your own path and observing where you go and why. Take charge and grab the reins of your own mind.

LEADERSHIP LESSON #4: EVERYONE HAS TO START SOMEWHERE

Steve Jobs and Steve Wozniak were prepared to make a company that would exceed the expectations of everyone around them. However, they found that creating a company couldn't just happen out of thin air, and the funds which they initially received were limited. Steve Jobs needed a place where they could build the Apple I, and in order to do this with the funds they had, they had to find a location to place their business in order to thrive with the sales they made. Where does a company start at the beginning of its life?

Steve's Solution

In order to create the company with the funds they had, Jobs and Wozniak humbly accepted their family garage as their designated place for business. A small garage was most definitely not the most reputable spot for a company to start, but Jobs and Wozniak knew that a company had to start somewhere, and in the long run, it wasn't the location and the fluff of a company that made them great, it was the performance of the products and services that were provided. With their set up ready, they created the company and designed the Apple I computer.

Any Company Starts with Humble Beginnings

No project can immediately start with gold ceilings and diamond walls. Company start-ups must be created with the funds available, and one of the last things on the mind of start-up CEO's are the location and prestige of the company's starting location. The focus should be on the products and on the services provided to the customers. A leader must understand that starting an idea and a project will be rocky and will come with a lot of challenges along the way. Jobs and Wozniak had much more to worry about than simply their place of business. They had a computer to build that would compete with the large corporations of IBM and PC.

In hindsight, what the company looks like at the beginning will not matter in the end, because what was created was the company itself. Many companies in today's modern world are successful, multi-million dollar companies that are created and still run in their own homes, with no special palace or office building required to match the success of the company. Jobs made a statement that he was willing to do anything to create his company by starting it in the garage of his home.

Summary

Pursuing your ideas and dreams will require a sense of humility, and the ability to do whatever it takes to achieve the things you seek. Being a leader means that you put the people you are serving first, and you take the inconveniencies in order to create the best possible product for people who purchase it. You need a heart to create things under your own duress, and the ability to take what little is given to you with the bigger picture in mind. Success starts small and ends in infinite value.

LEADERSHIP LESSON #5: LOOK SMARTER; NOT HARDER

While the computer technology industry was rapidly growing, the opportunities for stepping into the door of the industry were extremely narrow. Most people across the nation saw computers as chunky, expensive feats of magic and technology. Steve Jobs had to create a way for their company to be different, and to expose themselves into the markets in a way that would be remembered by the customers. What Jobs and Wozniak needed was a way to create their computers that would attract attention and make a brand for their companies that would stand out beyond the other companies in the industry.

Steve's Solution

Steve Jobs made the smart decision that most others in the industry didn't think to make. Instead of going with the wind of the other competitors and creating computers that were similar in fashion and technology, Jobs decided to brand against the wind and go a direction that his competitors didn't look to pursue. Jobs created computers that were smaller, not larger. He made computers that were cheaper, not more expensive. Finally Jobs made sure that the computer's design and function were intuitive and available to everyone.

Find the Solution that Others Don't

A big factor that goes into the success of an idea is whether or not the idea is wildly sought after. It's seen in many industries today that almost every company in the industry sells something generally similar to each other, and that not much innovation and creativity takes place. Instead of doing something against the path, and creating their own product that is unique to the competitors, most companies in each industry adopt the ideas and creations of others, and simply follow the path laid out for them.

While in certain instances this might be profitable, this is not what true leadership is about. Leadership requires making a path alone, and finding that niche in the market that is unseen by the competitors. There, innovation creates success, because of the uniqueness of the products in the market. Taking the initiative to look for smarter solutions will yield much more profit than fighting against an army of competitors to sell the same product. Although more work may go into finding that smart solution, the gains made by the hard work will far outweigh those of following the majority.

Summary

In order to fulfil the dreams that you have in your mind, it is required that you to go away from the stream of others, and instead focus on different ways to

27

solve similar problems. This is how entrepreneurs create their success, and it is how leaders innovate in everything they do. It takes an eye for identifying ways to create solutions that others have not created themselves, and with this special eye comes special attention from customers and competition alike. Pursue what is smarter for your ideas and your dreams, and do not let yourself get caught up in the actions of the majority.

LESSON #6: PROCESS OVER EVENT

Steve's creation of Apple Computers was an event that made him famous as an innovator and an entrepreneur. However, while his business was a wild success, and his fame and wealth rapidly accumulated, he was soon cast out of the company by his executive board. He was soon left with no claim to the company that he created with Wozniak, and had to make the decision to either give up on what he had lost, or pick the pieces up and continue on. Steve's event of Apple Computers was something phenomenal, but he had something greater: he had a process.

Steve's Solution

Jobs would not give up on his track of success that easily. While he was booted out of a company that he worked extremely hard for, he took with him the secret to the company's success. Jobs nearly didn't miss a beat, and he quickly started the NeXT Company and began his path with Pixar Animation Studios. How could it be that Steve Jobs could have created 3 successful companies in a row, while most people can't create a single thriving company? The answer is within the process, and Steve Job's process was one of the most successful in the industry.

Build Businesses on Process, not on Events

Dreamers want to be rich and famous, controlling a Fortune 500 company while wallowing in their success. However, those dreamers are missing 99% of the journey that it would take to get there. Jobs took years of hard work and diligence in order to make Apple Computers, and it was the hard work and diligence that made the company, not the products themselves.

Jobs was kicked out of Apple Computers, and Apple quickly began to deflate in its reputation and sales. Why? Because all that was left in the company was the event of its greatness, not the process of hard work and innovation that made the company great. While the product and branding can be a significant part of an idea's success, nothing will be more important than the process that the person takes to make that idea a reality. Jobs could have started a business in any industry, because he had the mind and process that would make anything a successful adventure.

Summary

So, you want to build something of great value with your idea? It will take a lot more than one day's work. It will take longer than a week. The purpose of success comes from the long timeline of hard work that it takes to build the success from the ground up. You can't have something of value easily, and in the midst of the large human population, ideas are nearly worthless. It is the person adopting the idea and the work ethic they carry that makes all the difference.

LESSON #7: PAY YOURSELF LAST

Jobs created the NeXT Company, which was purchased by his former company, Apple Computers. He soon took again his throne at Apple, and was left with the mess that the former executives had made of his company. He now had the task of reviving the strength of the company and dominating the industry against his competitor, IBM. He immediately went to work growing his company again, using his innovative skills to reshuffle the business. But his goal would take everything that he had, and it would require absolute concentration on Apple Computers.

Steve's Solution

Refusing to let his original company fail due to the decisions of others, Jobs gave everything he had in order to push for the company's survival. Injecting everything into the company, Job's was left on a personal yearly salary of $1. Committed to success, Jobs left himself unimaginably broke so that he could restore his company and create the great reputation that it once had. Because of his extreme loyalty to his company, his forced salary lead to the company's creation of the iMac, a product that accelerated the company's footing in the industry, and put his company back in the game.

You Must Give Everything to Get Everything

Jobs would not allow his temporary comfort to affect the future of his company. Apple Computers was controlled by a man who gave everything he had to see its success, and because of that decision, the company is now one of the largest and most profitable companies in the world. Smart decisions of self-sacrifice are the efforts it takes to create a great company from an idea, and there is no room for doubt or back-up plans. Jobs didn't believe in back-up plans, and to show his confidence, he put everything on the line.

An idea needs the confidence of its owner in order to survive. Any doubt will decrease its chance of success. It requires everything to be sacrificed in order for it to accelerate into a rapidly growing success. Small bets make small returns, but the more that is put into the pot, the larger the reward will be. It takes absolute assurance of the idea's success to make a sacrifice like Jobs did, and it takes a hardened leader to have the strength to make that decision for an idea. But a leader believes in the ideas that are created.

Summary

Companies cannot be created with a doubtful leader. You must have the ability to make sacrifices, and you must be willing to put everything into an idea, or it may not succeed. No matter what the idea is, or how much potential it holds, nothing will be accomplished if there is no weight put into its motion. To assure success, your leadership must create and offer something that is truly from everything that you have. Whether it be time, money, or both, an idea is a needy creature and it requires all of your attention to succeed.

LEADERSHIP LESSON #8: STRATEGICALLY SHARE SELECTIVELY

Jobs had created several big shot companies in his career, and had reached the peak of his fame in the world of business creators and entrepreneurs. However, his fame would soon become an obstacle that he would have to overcome. In 2003, Jobs discovered the Pancreatic Cancer that would eventually be his downfall, and this news scared more than just him and his family. A decision had to be made on how he would take this in accordance to the public, his family and his company.

Steve's Solution

A very traumatic event took place within the CEO of a highly successful company, news that was extremely sensitive to the public, especially investors. Jobs knew the secret would have to be kept, but to whom? And for how long? Due to his diagnosis, his disappearance from the scene of Apple Computers for a small time left people suspicious, and Jobs had to act quickly in a way that would leave everything at Apple Computers stable. His strategic selective sharing of his cancer to only certain people kept Apple Computers afloat, and his pancreatic cancer went unnoticed for some time.

Information is Valuable

What someone knows and when they know it is a crucial part of any walk through life. Curiosity spreads knowledge like fire, and the wrong information in a crowd can lead to destruction. In Job's case, he was pressed with a situation that could potentially become the downfall of his company. Should the investors had discovered Job's illness, backers and reputation that had given Apple its momentum might have come to a halt, causing the company to buckle under the weight. Sharing information in such a high profile world was an art that required precision.

When it comes to information, always have a strategy for who to share it with, and why. The purpose of information should always benefit the idea of a leader, and should never work against him. In order to preserve this, leaders need to be aware of the information that is known and shared within the network. Steve Jobs controlled the mouths of those he knew, and because of his leadership, his company continued to grow into the enormous corporation that it is now. Sharing selectively is a required skill in the business world.

Summary

Whether it be a secret ingredient, an incredible idea, or news about an illness, it is always a battle to keep and choose who should know the sensitive information. In a world of unpredictability, trends of success and of failure can start from a single share online, and news can spread across the world through the mouths of a few people and the internet. Be a mastermind of your team, and control the scene of being a celebrity by building your brand and keeping everything else out of the picture. This will create a successful image towards you and your idea, and leave the doubts of others out of sight.

LEADERSHIP LESSON #9: BE A TREND-SETTER

IBM was formerly one of the most unapproachable companies, and most other companies in the industry simply copied their magnificent operations in order to get a share of the profit that IBM made. It was known as nearly impossible back then to be able to compete with IBM, let alone beat them in their own industry. But Jobs was determined to make this a reality. How would he create a company that would break through the strong flow that IBM's trend had created within the industry? Job's decision made IBM obsolete.

Steve's Solution

IBM may have been a very powerful company, and arguably the most dominant in the industry. However, while companies were following in the footsteps of IBM, Jobs made the choice to do the exact opposite. Apple Computers was a company that went against IBM's computer design, and instead focused on creating their own trends through their systems and software. Because of this decision to go against the wind in the industry, Apple began to create its own current of popularity, and it caused the kind of tension that IBM had never had to deal with before. Apple had created a trend more powerful than the industry leader.

Create Your Own Path

All of the companies that competed with IBM using similar products and services were caught in a rat race. While they were increasing their share of the profits, they were only increasing in a share, while Apple Computer was making their own large chunk in the industry. Jobs created a trend, and pushed to make it more popular than IBM. It was the uniqueness of Apple Computers that made it stick out from the several other companies in the industry, and because of the continued trend setting, Apple is still the leading company in its industry.

Those who set trends are ahead of the game, and those that follow are simply followers. It takes a certain kind of leader to make the confident decision to make their own way towards a goal and set themselves apart as a competitor. It is brave, but dangerous. However, this decision is fruitful if it is done well, and the trend is meant to trump the old leading competitor's trend. Taking a stance as a leader of the industry, and replacing the competition with new and improved publicity will cause the race to be in the favor of the new trend setter.

Summary

Competition is all about who the better competitor is, and it is not exclusive to one ability or trait. You don't have to simply improve upon a former

39

trend to be successful. Rather, setting your own trend and making your idea completely unique and different from the competition will be a factor that substantially increases your visibility, and strengthens your brand in a way that will allow you to climb above the competition and stick out as a leader in your industry!

LEADERSHIP LESSON #10: PERSONAL LIFE LEADERSHIP

Steve Jobs went on to create some of the most successful companies in their industries, and make a net worth for himself that tops the list in the United States. His ventures were great, and his legacy set in stone, but the life of a man goes beyond his business journey. Jobs dealt with personal life issues that constantly plagued him as he made his way to the top, and as he became more successful, he spent more and more effort on trying to fix the relationship with his family.

Steve's Solution

Steve understood the importance of his personal relationships in his later years, and he pursued repairing his relationship with his daughter that he did not accept as his own until she was 7 years old. Steve knew that he had made a mistake by prioritizing his business life over his personal life, and it was a mistake that he had to repair. The daughter that had taken him so long to accept came to live with him when she became a teenager, and his time was spent on more than just his successful company.

Business is Not All in Life

While Jobs did not understand this lesson until later in his life, it became very clear to him how important this was. Abandoning a family in pursuit of success is not a decision that a leader makes. Family and relationships with others should be balanced along with the hard work that is put in to the creation of an idea. Striving to become a better father made Steve Jobs a stronger leader, and helped him in the future as he continued to fight the difficult battle of pancreatic cancer.

Leaders lift up those around him, and always look out for the better interests of the people that he loves. This is important, because business pursuits can corrupt a leader and make him greedy and lose heart in the things that he should care for the most. Staying strong with the family, and understanding the importance of supporting those around the business adventure, will enable a leader to grow within himself, and become a stronger person. Being successful is a pinnacle greatness to achieve, but a leader cannot do it alone, and he should never do it to the destruction allow the lives of others.

Summary

Leadership goes beyond simply achieving great things. Accomplishments only go so far in defining your identity and reputation as a successful person, and everyone must have a rock to lean on in times of hardship. Jobs pursued his family so hard in the end, because he realized how much of a mistake he made in not pursuing those relationships earlier on. Your wealth will be a big factor in your happiness, but a life is not well lived without the love of a family, and the support of a network that is cared for.

CONCLUSION

The success and legacy of Steve Jobs required a lifetime of strategic decisions and hard work. No multi-billion dollar company can be created overnight. Being a leader for a great idea takes more, and the determination that you have is a necessity for success. Steve Jobs created his wealth through these lessons that he held within himself, and his natural ability to take advantage of these attributes made him one of the richest men in the world.

While Jobs was a great man, and held great attributes that take most people years of practice to form within themselves, the same amount of success can be brought to you if you take these leadership lessons to heart and learn how to integrate them into a lifestyle. Daily meditation on these 10 elements of success will bring you towards your goals, and will grow your ideas much further than you've ever imagined. Steve Jobs once started out in the same position as you are standing now, and the difference between you and Jobs is the dedication he took to make his dreams happen.

Just as he began, you can begin too, and really mold yourself as a leader that can take a process and turn it into successful events that will mark your place in history. Being an entrepreneur does not make you a leader, and it is important to remember that leadership is not defined by success, it is simply a product of leadership. Understanding these factors will bring you to a better understanding of yourself, and you will see yourself come closer to your dreams, and to the people that you love. Leaders must hold these attributes in every area of their life, and cannot allow themselves to be too wrapped up in the business world.

When Steve Jobs passed away, he left behind more than just his enormous accumulation of wealth and his terrifically successful companies. Jobs left behind an essence of leadership that will be missed by millions of people. He left behind shoes that will never be filled. Steve Jobs created his own definition of a leader, and because of these legendary lessons he left behind, others can learn to make their own successes and define themselves among the community of leaders within the business world.

You hold the same potential that the late Steve Jobs held. All it takes is the decision and the commitment to pursue these foundations for leadership. The next great success in the world could sprout from your mind, and your wildest dreams could become a reality amongst the stars because of your decision to pursue leadership. Possess a deep understanding of the events that lead Steve Jobs to becoming an enormous success, and you may find yourself possessing your own events of enormous success. It all starts with a change in you.

BOOKS FROM MICHAEL WINICOTT

Another titles by Michael Winicott you may find interesting:

BILL GATES: BUSINESS LESSONS

BRAIN: EXERCISES TO EMPOWER

BUSINESS PLAN: A practical guide

FACEBOOK MARKETING: Business Lessons from Mark Zuckerberg

HABITS: MICRO CHANGES for MACRO RESULTS

HENRY FORD: ENTERPRENEURSHIP LESSONS

JESUS: LEADERSHIP LESSONS

LEONARDO DA VINCI: CREATIVITY LESSONS

MARTIN LUTHER KING: LIFE LESSONS

OPRAH WINFREY: LIFE LESSONS

WALT DISNEY: CREATIVITY LESSONS

WINSTON CHURCHILL: LEADERSHIP LESSONS

DID YOU ENJOY THIS BOOK?

Thanks for purchasing and reading this book. If you reached this page you had probably enjoyed it. Would you care to leave a positive review in Amazon?

This is very important for 2 reasons:

a) I need your feedback to improve the quality of my books

b) Other people may read and benefit from this book if you share your thoughts.

Thanks a lot for providing your review!

Michael Winicott